T0104747

Dangerous Pastime

Ekpe Inyang

Langaa Research & Publishing CIG
Mankon, Bamenda

Publisher:
Langaa RPCIG
Langaa Research & Publishing Common Initiative Group
P.O. Box 902 Mankon
Bamenda
North West Region
Cameroon
Langaagrp@gmail.com
www.langaa-rpcig.net

Distributed in and outside N. America by African Books Collective
orders@africanbookscollective.com
www.africanbookscollective.com

ISBN: 9956-763-36-5

DISCLAIMER
All views expressed in this publication are those of the author and do
not necessarily reflect the views of Langaa RPCIG.

Table of Contents

iv

"The best way to understand a people
is to live with the people;
the best way to live with the people
is to share with the people, and
the best thing to share with the people
is what the people need."

Ekpe Inyang, 1992

I Have Rights!
20 December 2011

I

It's true he sent for her
Actually not her but anyone, even her, in a raving
moment
But then the meeting resulted in nothing
And for almost a fruiting season and a half
He neither dreamt nor thought of her

Nothing of that encounter
Warranted his memory of her
Albeit to her the occasion seemed to mean
At least the cultivation of a fertile piece of land
Then one peaceful day she rang to inform

She was around the corner waiting for him
But why? he asked
Have you forgotten so soon? she retorted
Forgotten what? Then on second thought he said to
himself
Just receive her and find her a place to stay the night

Give her what she needs but yield not to her intent
And help her find the road the very next day
But he was wrong, she wouldn't let him go!
How easily he was forced abed to stay the night
Beside her against his will for a full, long night

Dripping with sweat all night long
Occasionally panting, palpitating with fear
He had broken the oath
That divine covenant made,
With his better-half, on the alter

II

In just a few days after that night
He got a ring to tell him in a tone so harsh
A tone that made him develop a culprit's heart
Send me green notes quick
To do away with it

Do away with what?
Forgotten that it burst?
Send it quick before the problem mounts!
What language is that?
No more questions - this calls for no delay!

Send it not in my name
But in a name I now send
Tang-tang-tang, tang-tang, tang-tang!
Came the message, causing him to tremble
And he sent the money without further questions

Time elapsed, many, many moons waved goodbye
Then came a ring one quiet afternoon
Hi, Daddy, I miss you so much!
Sure you do?
Sure! How can we meet? I'm just around the corner

I am…I am…I am out of town!
Okay, send me transport and let me go
Send you what?
Transport money. I have dropped my test-pen, and am
franc-less
Completely broke, to say the least

No means where I am for such transaction
What then do I do?
How did you come…? Mean how did you get there?
What question is that?

It's a question that demands a genuine answer!

III

The very next day
Came another ring
I'm now back at home!
How did you make it?
Never mind; keep it for another time

Three months later
Came yet another ring
On my way to school - how can we meet?
I don't know, really
You don't care – simply tell me you don't!

Filled with guilt, he called to arrange they met
By a filling station
To give her the money
Since she said she was sick
And badly needed drugs

The money she took
And went her way
Since he was in no mood
For another night
Good bye! and she waved back to him

IV

More frequent rings
Then one day he found himself
Around the corner, and she rang as if she knew
Where are you?
Around the corner, said he unintentionally!

Now no good excuse
Why they shouldn't meet
And she came right where he was
Complaining she was sick again
Yet decided to stay the night

How can I get the drugs?
That was early the next day
Broke I am right now was his response
But in two days I should pay
And he was woken by a ring early that morning

V
Many moons came and went
Not a single ring
Then came one that bright day
Asking for transport money again
To take her home, after the exams-fever
In the field right now
Where no such transaction is possible
I will wait until you're back, then
Telling me your sponsor can't afford to pay?
What question is that?

And just the next day came another ring
You forgot you had a wife when you called for me?
And now you dared insult my family?
Insult? Me? How did I do it?

You did pour insults, and shall regret the act!

And in just a few days came yet another ring
I'm right where you are! Taking me for a fool?
He couldn't figure out what this meant
And on she went, By tomorrow I'll trace you...
And you'll know I have rights!
Which forced an eddy current up his head

Just Yesterday
11 February 2013

Just yesterday
On my way to the field
Three colleagues with me
At dusk now drizzling
Between Loum and Nkongsamba
At a sharp bend, a devil's elbow
Suddenly shot in a truck
Wobbling uncontrollably
Down a steep hill
Then took a sudden veer
Blocking our way fully
Rendering us helpless
And about to crush our car
And our stunned selves
In its steel chassis
But immediately it swerved again, taking our lane
And hitting an earthen wall on the tarred road

In a big bang, its face turned looking where it came
Giving a clear way for our car to take its lane
Which, with the help of that unseen, merciful hand
Manoeuvres its way out of the scene in time to save our
lives

Drama Defined
5 September 2013

Drama is drama in drama,
A re-enactment of real or imagined life,
Events presented as hyperbole or hypobole,
Served in a fine dish of dialogue and action,
Facilitating digestion,
Creating scintilating sparks for accurate guesses
Point the way to likely ending;
This not only by the renditions of characters,
More from their individual and collective actions;
And, as note of caution,
We are, by nature, actors and actresses
Displaying on an ever-widening stage of life,
Watched by three pairs eyes:
Spec-actors, spectators, and repor-actors.

High Is The Tide
10 August 2013

Great is the time
That makes it mine
High is the tide
That does not hide
Go on a ride
Run from the bite
Pick up a bike
Ignore the hike

So Clear And Dear
15 September 2013

Let not your heart
Be gripped by fear
Now that you hear
Something so dear

Come now and bear
The message clear
Like a joyful tear
Wetting my beard

Looking Back
15 September 2013

Looking back
At that quiet moment
When all I could
Was lie and suck
Thank God now tall I stand
A golden badge on suit

Looking back
At that great moment
When all I could
Was lie and scream
Thank God now tall I stand
A golden staff in hand

Looking back
At that sweet moment
When all I could
Was lie and smile
Thank God now tall I stand
A golden crown on head

Humans Still Without Rationality!?!
14 March 2014

Conflicts – backbiting
Quarrels, disputes, hijacking,
Terrorism, open wars –
Basic, negative animal expressive instincts
Still rife in and between human communities!?!
Confirming humans as still
At the basic stage in the evolutionary journey!?!
Humans advanced in science and technology
But still without suggestive rationality!?!
Humans still bent on sponsorship of missions
– Still clinging to development of technologies –
Of mass destruction to nullify current mass
construction!?!

What Do I...?
14 March 2014

What do I see,
Standing by the sea?

What do I hear,
Sleeping by the bear?

What do I hold,
Coming to be told?

What do I sense
From message so dense?

Song Of A Baby
16 March 2014

Tell the lion
Lie on

And the python
Pry on

Say to the chicken
Chip in

But not to weevil
Wee ill

The Clever Thief
24 March 2014

Came he in the darkest hour
Under an utterly unruly sky broke he in
Hiding weapons in display of clean hands

Each of a line of houses
Raked he, aided by unknown gang
A lot of goodies in store, glued they to the act

Satisfied, finally, it was time the scene to leave
But just on the first step out with the loads
Darkness to bright daylight gave way

Surrounding houses now agape
Occupants streaming out the scene to view
Suddenly shouted he, running as he did:

Thief, thief, thief, finger in front pointing
At no one in view, attention from him to draw
Running and running and running from the scene

Imitation And Immigration
8 May 2014

Imitation
Has some limitation
Like immigration
Unlike emigration

Adaptation
Has some limitation
Like mitigation
Unlike mutation

Plantation
Has some limitation
Like deforestation
Unlike eutrophication

Production
Has some limitation
Like reproduction
Unlike repercussion

Nothing Wrong
27 May 2014

Expressing a personal opinion,
Nothing wrong;

Maintaining one's position,
Nothing wrong;

Steering towards a particular direction;
Nothing wrong;

Taking a certain initiative,
Nothing wrong;

Condemning a particular initiative,
Nothing wrong;

Taking a particular decision,
Nothing wrong;

Doing so for selfish reasons,
Something definitely wrong.

Since…
28 May 2014

Man has been on earth
Since…

Has been feasting on it
Since…

Has been using it to develop sophisticated technologies
Since…

Has been struck by the impact of his poor treatment of it
Since…

Has been figuring out how best to ameliorate the situation
Since…

Thieving Rain
27 June 2014

Friday
It touched the ground
Pounding
Left the land flooding
Pushed the Sun to the front
Slept behind snoring
Refusing
It ever came out of its bed
That day

Power Of Knowledge
27 July 2014

Enlightened generations survive the worst storms of
time;
Knowledge lights the winding tunnel of confusion;
People deprived of it get trapped in the abyss of demise;
Every civilisation must take cupfuls of it to persist.

Internalise this message and spare yourself regrets;
Never minimise the power of the word
You receive from the trembling voice of the old;
And think of the fountain that heals us of all ills;
No civilisation ever can
Grow surely without feasting on the nutrients of history.

Cruel Thoughts
27 July 2014

Cruel thoughts
Crawling into cruel hearts
Cruel hearts
Creating cruel visions
Cruel visions
Creating cruel weapons
Cruel weapons
Crushing humankind
Cruel guns
Cruel bombs
Cruel missiles
Cruel drones
Creation of cruel thoughts

Caring To Better The World
27 July 2014

When genuine love shall be shared again
And hatred be treated with disdain
Then shall the world see unending peace
And our lips shall no longer sigh
And our hearts shall no longer tremble
And our vision shall no longer be blurred

When our sense of unity shall be rekindled
And division be seen as a spiteful act
Then shall we build and not later destroy
And our lips shall no longer sigh
And our hearts shall no longer tremble
And our vision shall no longer be blurred

When our spirit of care shall be born again
And killing be seen not even in dreams
Then shall we share and better the world
And our lips shall no longer sigh
And our hearts shall no longer tremble
And our vision shall no longer be blurred

They Send Us
27 July 2014

They send us to steal instead of give;
To intimidate instead of console;
To kill instead of protect;
To destroy instead of build.

They give us rods instead of roots;
Bullets instead of grains;
Guns instead of staffs;
Bombs instead of balls.

They teach us darkness instead of light;
Cruelty instead of kindness;
Tragedy instead of comedy;
War instead of peace.

They make us starve in the bush instead of feast at home;
Angry with brethren instead of happy with them;
Despondent instead of hopeful;
Commit suicide instead of stay alive.

Still Too Young To Imagine How
28 July 2014

He went to school in a city,
Faraway land across the seas,
And wears the biggest hat over the largest robe;
But he's still too young to imagine how.

He never spent a day with grandfather,
And can't tell the smell of an old loin-cloth,
Nor the feel of a red turban;
He's still too young to imagine how.

He's so fond of gas and electric cookers, or microwaves,
But can't picture the three-stone stove with fuel-wood
Spouting out jets of smoke to feed his mum's lungs;
He's still too young to imagine how.

He talks generously about crackers and wines,
But can't describe the taste of kola-nuts;
Nor the smell of palm-wine;
He's still too young to imagine how.

He talks of medicine stores,
But can hardly identify a herb
Let alone explain its use;
He's still too young to imagine how.

He can tell the speed of a Mercedes Benz,
But can't compare it with that of a leopard,
Let alone describe a tortoise's pace;
He's still too young to imagine how.

He describes stadia lanes with expertise,
But has no hint about foot-beaten forest tracks,
Nor any idea about the village square;

He's still too young to imagine how.

He gives long lectures on Einstein's works,
Like Stephen Hawking spins out the theory of everything,
But cannot decipher the mystery behind
The gyrating power of ndeem, the snake masquerade
That grows taller than Kororp coconut trees
And then shorter than tea plants at Tole;
He's still too young to imagine how.

Listen, Grand Daddy
31 July 2014

Oh, Grand Daddy
Listen to your grandson's plea
Listen to the counsel of the young
Devoid they are not of vision

Give Daddy a chance
Let him put on the red turban
Handle the broom
And do the libations

Grand Daddy
Your hand now trembles
Your voice quivering
When you perform the rites

Your gait
Sings your years
Your diction now
Too distant to comprehend

Oh, Grand Daddy, spare me the shame
Hand the broom, before the walls of docile patience
Come collapsing
Into the catacomb of molten wrath

The Red Turban
31 July 2014

They sat me
On the ancient stool
Engraved with leopards, elephants, eagles

They put me on
The regalia
Coated with blots from ancestral skins

They placed on my head
The red turban
Studded with seven red feathers of sacred birds

They handed me
The family staff
Great Granddaddy could not dare touch

They blessed me with the regal broom
Not for flies to whisk
But for evil spirits to ward off

Then on
My drinking glass has been
A mug made of uncommon material

My jar
Has seen less of air
And more of palm-wine

My throat
Has downed less of food and water
And more of kola-nut and palm-wine

Train To Gain
31 July 2014

Rain,
Train
His brain
To despise the sprain,
To endure the pain
As we set out to train;
To bring us pride of gain.

Every weakness now drain;
Beware any form of strain,
Let alone stain;
Let's in the rain
Harvest the grain;
Le's train
In rain to gain.

Enigmatic Defeat
31 July 2014

Enigmatic 2014 defeat
Though,
Organically prepared he was even for
Olympics.

Feel free, just
Imagine how disappointed
Lion was,
Sitting and watching

Several goals rushed in
After a few
Minutes of his injury, spectators in rain without
Umbrellas over their heads, still expectant,
Even after the first few goals
Landed on the net in lightning speed.

Bundles Of Secrets
1 August 2014

Murmurings in conversation
Faint clouds during condensation
Undeclared culls in conservation
Bundles of secrets

Faintest strokes in a painting
Unknown particles for tainting
Major news items tailing
Bundles of secrets

Partially declared wealth
Broken speeches in a breath
Unwritten will upon death
Bundles of secrets

The forbidden river
The masked diver
The unseen tiger
Bundles of secrets

Mask behind the face
Interludes in a race
Truncated phase
Bundles of secrets

Free Yourself
20 August 2014

Free yourself from
Every form of yoke;
Lead a life dictated by that small
Internal voice divine,
True,
Immaculate
And pure.

Enlighten every
Nation
In

Ethics of
True nationhood, devoid of
Internal strife and guided by
Mutual respect and protection.

Closing Up Ugly Gaps
(Inspired by an Anointed Man of God)
24 August 2014

A pool of germs
Smelling for orifices,
Fractures,
Ruptured skin,
The body to invade;

A sea of demons
Detecting vain desires,
Evil plans,
Weaknesses,
The soul to colonize.

The body to protect,
Keep sacrosanct
The orifices;
Close up, completely heal
The fracture, the ruptured skin;

The soul to save,
Disdain, completely destroy
The vain desire,
The evil plan,
The overt or covert weakness.

Penchant For Blood
25 August 2014

The orb of life has gone amok
Constructing Jacuzzis of wrath
Conducting workshops of carnage
Even against innocent juveniles
Strolling the streets in play

The well of bestiality
Keeps her mouth agape
Sucking up
At dawn, at noon, at dusk, at night
Young innocent blood

The spirit of vengeance
Roams the streets
Visiting temples, synagogues
Churches, mosques, every
House of worship, ruining souls

Whirlwinds rule the sky
Hurling capsules of demolition
At dawn, at noon, at dusk, at night
Ravaging cities
Murdering even infants in sweet sleep

The spirit of retribution
Crowns every head
Like the mad cow disease
Herds of grazing cows
Now nose-bleeding

Spreading freely
The contagious disease
Region to region

Breaking barricades
Despising sovereignty

The sky wears petals of gore
Signifying the need for vaccines
This time surely not against malaria
And HIV and Ebola but to slay
The growing penchant for blood

Dangerous Pastime
26 August 2014

A siren and a rain of blasts,
And they scurried up the stairs,
Hid behind an iron door
Multiple-bolted and barred,
And peeping through a hole in the left window,
Dubanzi, refusing to be party, this time
Watched them, from the height,
Engaged in that dangerous pastime,
Marching, walking, running
Through the streets,
Dashing into the woods,
Skulking between houses,
Pressed against the walls
In long, winding queues,
Like giant snakes
In outfits of green,
Wrapped in capsule-like beads,
Holding weird staffs
Pointing to the front,
Marching, walking, running,
Searching, hopping,
Sweaty bodies
Exuding boiling anger,
Ready for another carnage,
Damage and looting,
Dismantling the frame of peace.

Thirst In The Desert
29 August 2014

Thirsty in the desert,
Their complaints building up,
Their anger rising high
Against their leader,
Against their Saviour,
Against their Master,
Despite the obvious fact
Liberated they were from
Centuries of bondage.
Met they, in that tired state,
A hard, dry rock
At that familiar Mount
As resting place,
No hope
Their thirst to quench,
Their anger soaring higher
Against their leader,
Against their Saviour,
Against their Master.
Harkening to the voice,
That divine command,
The rock the leader struck
With the saving rod,
Yet their anger he provoked
All the more, as, to them,
A big joke it was
Striking the dry rock,
When water it was
All they needed.
But lo! a gush of pure water
In no time flowing,
Their ageing thirst to quench,
Their rising anger

To suppress,
Their leader's burdened head to save,
Another lesson to learn,
Their Master's undying,
Abundant saving grace to trust.

Will Surely Drain
31 August 2014

Train
Your brain
To hoard the gain;
No matter how much rain,
The porous soil'll surely drain.

Redemption Day
1 September 2014

Today we have submitted ourselves unto
Our Lord, Jesus Christ, the only Saviour and

Guarantor of the abundance of life, the
Omnipresent, omniscient and omnipotent God who, by
His
Divine interventions, unending protection, and infinite
mercies, has

Bountifully blessed us, providing us with
Everything we need today, tomorrow and the days
thereafter.

To Him, indeed, everything is possible, as
Here we bring testimonies of what, some years ago, we
couldn't,
Even in our wildest dreams, consider as foreseeable
achievements.

Glory be to you, Almighty God, as you continue to show
us that great
Love, the only instrument we need to truly and effectively
Overpower all principalities and powers,
Restoring blessings stolen by our enemies, breaking away
from their
Yoke and tribulations, and receiving your salvation
forever and ever.

Green Campaign
16 September 2014

Enlightened rural children
Speak out against
Destruction of forests

Until
NGOs of the South
Enter into
Solar energy deals with
Companies
Overseas.

Can these
Organisations of green views
Not only widely distribute but
Train the rural communities
In its proper use in order
Not to
Undermine the need for
Energy
Saving and proper disposal?

Heart Of Gold Or Heart Of Tar

(Adapted from my Facebook post of 12 March 2014)
25 September 2014

Hearts of Gold:
Embers,
Torchlights in the dark;

Hearts of Tar:
Dreadful shadows,
Overwhelming clouds in daylight.

Yours is the choice
Which heart to wear,
Each heart
Yielding its own fruit.

Give And Take

(Based on an African tale)
25 September 2014

A kingdom in the distant past
The king had passed a law
Any man seen publicly
Slapping his body
To kill or scare mosquitoes
Should be hanged

His eyes were on a beautiful girl
Staying near his palace
Was afraid men who came visiting
So frequently were potential poachers
Hence every one of such visitors
Was escorted to a public toilet
Known to house a city of mosquitoes

Many a handsome male visitor
Had lost their lives
And then came the turn of Tortoise
Who was so familiar with the story
And had been decrying the death toll
He decided to draw its curtain

Tortoise consulted a make-up specialist
Who molded and transformed him into
The handsomest young man
The human eye had ever beheld
And organized a trip to that kingdom
Guarded by seven beautiful young women
Purporting to be a prince visiting
The most beautiful girl in that kingdom
After introducing himself and his mission

Tortoise indicated he would like to use a bathroom
And the king arranged for his guards
To show him to the public toilet
And Tortoise left his bodyguards behind
And followed the king's guards
To the public toilet
Armed with a tale strategy

While taking care of himself at the toilet
Under the watchful eyes of the king's guards
Tortoise told one of the most famous stories
A story about a spotted cow
That belonged to a king in a distant land

As the mosquitoes swarmed him
Tortoise boldly slapped the spots
Where they were biting him
Under the guise of illustrating his story:
"Spots on the face, spots on the neck,
Spots on the hand, spots on the leg…"
This to the entertainment of the king's guards
Who went to the palace happily with the report
"Tortoise is such an extraordinary man
Who bears the disturbing bites without flinching"

The king was crossed
And ordered them back to the scene
To see him supervise the exercise himself
Accompanied by members of his Palace Council
To watch the show and while at the toilet
Tortoise still told his story with even more dexterity
And at some point invited
The king to "Come and see…"
The king walked closer to behold the spots
Tortoise was describing whereupon
Mosquitoes poured on him
And bit him so badly

He slapped every part of his body
Uncontrollably, hence pronouncing
Publicly the cruel penalty on himself

The Executor
25 September 2014

Works he in a distant land
His sword over his homeland
Just because of shit cash
Or to defend some bizarre creed

Wears he a hood from head to toe
His skin and face to conceal
Tries even his voice to twist
But the effort his accent clearly slayed

Sees he his people with two clear eyes
Talks to them in familiar accent
Yet takes off their crowns one by one
His part to play in the deal

How long must the play shake the stage
His leading part to execute
How soon will the curtain be drawn his hood stripped off
His face to face the light his sword to find a lasting sheath

Fight Not To Be
30 September 2014

Cotton during harvest
Lead during planting

Cheetah at instructions
Snail at propping the tasks

Sheep in the dress
Wolf in the chest

Donkey in the eyes
Tortoise in the head

Pig in the party
Ant in the field

Bat in the day
Owl in the night

Cat in the pool
Dog in the manger

Dolphin in aqua-theatre
Shark in the sea

Dove on the table
Snake under the chair

Fight not to be
Scorpion that bites its tail

Unknown Matter
4 October 2014

So he is **H**ere so sure
Albeit he w**A**s yester-years
Never so **R**igorous
Ready to **D**rive out

Let**T**ing
Math**A**r live
All a**L**one
To learn un**K**nown matter

Horror!
4 October 2014

Rockets flying,
Rocking
East to West,
West to East,
Wailing creating plangent
Air waves rising high,
Screaming
Amidst chaos,
Horror,
Pain and agony,
Pleading for help,
A thousand torsos,
Members tossed and lost,
Sprawling in red pools.

Rising Confusion
8 October 2014

    So much attraction
To more destruction
And such distraction
From real construction
    When boar constrictor
Stands as contractor
The co-detractor
Will bend the factor
    Devoid of passion
Dry of compassion
Good at collusion
Pads of coercion
    Rising confusion
In such diversion
Much less discussion
Makes good conclusion
    When in perfection
They see deception
And in redemption
They read temptation
    Push for invention
They view infection
Take one injection
They get dejection
    Blinding confusion
Cryptic delusion
Fetch them revulsion
Pay for derision

That's No Friend
9 October 2014

To know who you work with, sit with, eat with,
Chat with, laugh with, dance with, live with,
Be a brilliant student of Orature;
And if, in any passing moment,
You decipher, without an iota of doubt, that
Selfishness, greed, spite and jealousy,
Hypocrisy, callousness, hate and cruelty
Celebrate the diction,
Read the mission, then draw
And picture it clearly on the wall of your heart
That's no friend.
     To know who you work with, sit with, eat with,
Chat with, laugh with, dance with, live with,
Be a clever student of Visage-ology;
And if, in any passing moment,
You decipher, without an iota of doubt, that
Selfishness, greed, spite and jealousy,
Hypocrisy, callousness, hate and cruelty
Calibrate every contour,
Read the mission, then draw
And picture it boldly on the wall of your heart
That's no friend.
To know who you work with, live with, eat with,
Sleep with, chat with, laugh with, dance with,
Be an exceptional student of Psychoanalysis;
And if, in any passing moment,
You decipher, without an iota of doubt, that
Those traits dominate the output of your analysis,
Read the mission, then draw
And picture it permanently on the wall of your heart
That's no friend.

Breaking Predicaments
10 October 2014

Tear the dark
With blazing eyes
See beyond
The darkest cloud

Break the rock
With Moses' rod
Cross the sea
With utmost pluck

Let dawn see
You across the sea
And the Sun
Your head under a roof

Let your back see
The sea only with you across
And your front
Only before you cross

Dream of Baby Clinton
10 October 2014

I've played not
The game before
Know not the rules
Have not the skills
Nor the connections
But the strong desire
And vision
I'm born not for
The Third Division Club
Nor the Second Division Club
Nor the First Division Club
But the National Team
And whatever it takes
However long it lasts
I believe as I bow
In fervent supplication
I'll belong there by and by

Waiting To See Me Fall
11 October 2014

Waiting to see me fall
He spread
Cancerous tales on my head
But this time
It was my turn to be vindicated

Waiting to see me fall
He built
A censorious hut as my abode
But this time
It was my turn to find a castle

Waiting to see me fall
He fashioned
A gaping tunnel under my walkway
But this time
It was my turn to rise

My head was crowned with a hat of vindication
His hands adorned with cuffs of conviction
As I escaped his hellish, scornful hut
He was brutally flung into a rancid dungeon
Mine is an enviable throne, his the yawning tunnel

Now, Receive!
11 October 2014

    You make us
Walk the streets
Morning to night
You chauffeur-driven

    You show us
A grubby, public latrine
And use
A flushing toilet

    You make us
Work in rain and sun
Ordering us from
A pouched bureau

    You spray foul spittle
Into our eyes and ears and mouths
Give us names less than "beast!"
Only you a towering eagle

    You change the rules
Unchallenged
With unusual impunity
In the middle of the game

    You serve us
Dishes of scorpions
And feast on
A plate of lobsters

Now, receive
An earful
A staggering, scornful push
A rain of ousting blows

Where Do We Come From?
12 October 2014

The light we see here and now
Had existed billions of years ago,
Tearing through void and darkness and came
Travelling through time and space.

The scenes we see here and now
Were played billions of years ago,
In similar forms and details,
In familiar time and space.

Admittedly, our present us
Had existed billions of years ago,
Saying what we say today
Doing exactly what we do.

To conclude, grandchild, life, as we live it here and now,
Like drama, defined as an imitation of real life,
Is a replay of events enacted, at the birth of time,
On the palms of Alpha and Omega.

Printed in the United States
By Bookmasters